TIME

Published by Evans Brothers Limited
2A Portman Mansions
Chiltern Street
London W1M 1LE

British Library Cataloguing in Publication Data.
A catalogue record for this book is available from the British Library.

First published 1995
Reprinted 1996

Printed in Hong Kong by Wing King Tong Co. Ltd

ISBN 0 237 51586 5 (paperback)

Acknowledgements

Editorial: Rachel Cooke
Design: Ann Samuel
Production: Jenny Mulvanny
Photography: Michael Stannard
Consultant: Peter Patilla, formerly Senior Lecturer in mathematics education, Sheffield Hallam University
Artwork: Clinton Banbury Associates and Kathy Baxendale (pages 14 and 29)

The author and publishers would like to thank the following companies for their help with the objects photographed for this book:

Polydron International Ltd, clock on front cover and pages 24 and 25 (the digits showng the hours normally appear on the outer ring but were replaced by the digits for the minutes for the purposes of this book) (clock available from Polydron International Ltd, Kemble, Cirencester, Gloucestershire GL7 6BA); John Lewis Partnership, pages 8, 9, 11, 12, 13, 15, 16, 18, 20, 21, 26, 27 and 28; NES Arnold Limited, pages 9, 24 and 25; Tridias, 6 Bennett Street, Bath, BA1 2QP, 0225 314730, pages 9, 10, 11, 17, 18, 19, 22 and 27; Which Watch, pages 19 and 28.

For permission to reproduce copyright material the author and publishers gratefullly acknowledge the following:

Page 10: (mouse and fox) Hans Reinhard/Bruce Coleman Limited, (moth) Andrian Davies/Bruce Coleman Limited, (bat) Frank Greenaway/Bruce Coleman Limited. **Page 16:** (bottom left) Robert Harding Picture Library, (bottom right) Robert Bosch Domestic Appliances Limited. **Page 17:** (top left and bottom right) Robert Harding Picture Library, (centre left) Sony. **Page 19:** (top right) Robert Bosch Domestic Appliances Limited. **Page 25:** Robert Harding Picture Library.

Take off with

TIME

Sally Hewitt

Evans

Evans Brothers Limited

About this book

The activities, puzzles and games in this book about time have been designed for an adult and child to enjoy together. Take a while over the pages and enjoy finding out the many opportunities they provide for learning about time and how we measure it.

Each page deals with a topic that children will be introduced to in the early years at school. The pictures are of familiar objects and everyday situations that will help children to realise that time is not just about clocks, but that it is an important part of life. Children learn most effectively by joining in, talking, asking questions and solving problems, so encourage them to talk about what they are doing and to find ways of solving the problems for themselves.

The games and activities in the 'Take Off' loops will give children a chance to practise and develop the new skills they have been introduced to on that page. You may find it helpful to carry out the 'Take Off' activity on page 29, **Make a clock**, before you look at those pages concerned with telling the time.

Use the book as a starting point. Look for other opportunities to learn about time, for example, pointing out clocks when you are at the shops, seeing how long daily tasks take and noting the time of favourite television programmes. Make sure that it is not only easy to take off with time but also fun!

Contents

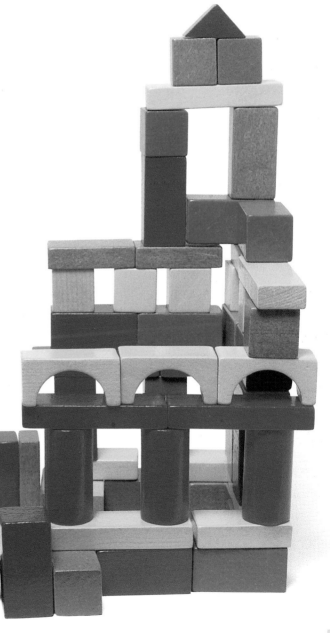

Daytime

Daytime begins when the sun rises in the morning.
It ends when the sun sets in the evening.
Use the pictures to find out what Joey does in a day.

Morning is the first part of the day.
What does Joey do in the morning?

Midday is the middle of the day.
Joey has his lunch at midday. What else does he do?

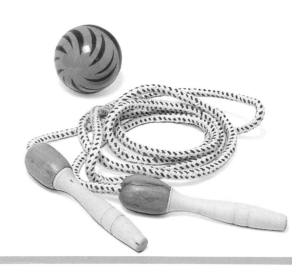

Afternoon comes between lunch time and evening.
What does Joey do after
painting his picture?

Evening is the end of the day.
What is the last thing Joey does in the evening?

My day

What did you do today?

Draw pictures
of things you
did today.

Make sure
you put them
in the right order.

He goes to bed.

Night-time

Night-time begins when the sun sets
and it gets dark.
Sometimes the moon and
stars come out.
Night-time ends when the sun
rises again in the morning.

At night, you go to
sleep after a busy day.
But not everyone
is sleeping.

Some animals look for food at night.

Some people work all night.

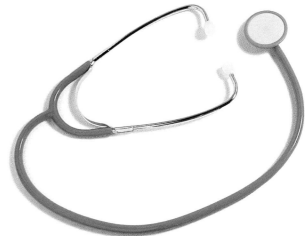

Who works at night to get these things ready for the morning?

Days of the week

There are 7 days in a week.
Do you know the names of the days of the week?

These pictures show you what Joey is doing this week.

 swimming

 going to
school

going to
the park

going to a party

visiting a friend

Monday	 
Tuesday	 
Wednesday	 

Thursday			
Friday			
Saturday			
Sunday			

Saturday and Sunday are called the weekend. Can you guess why?

The day today

What day is it today?
What is Joey doing today?
What did he do yesterday?
What is he going to do tomorrow?
Pretend another day is 'today' and ask the same questions.

Ask the same questions about yourself.

A year

In a year there are
365 days,
52 weeks,
12 months.

Every 4 years, a year is
a day longer.
It has 366 days.
We call this a leap year.

This year circle shows the names of the 12 months
and how long they are. It also shows the 4 seasons.

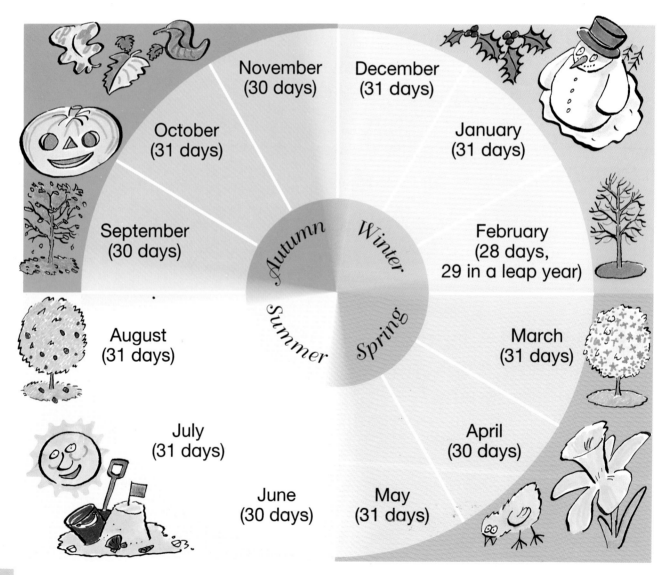

November
(30 days)

December
(31 days)

October
(31 days)

January
(31 days)

September
(30 days)

Autumn

Winter

February
(28 days,
29 in a leap year)

August
(31 days)

Summer

Spring

March
(31 days)

July
(31 days)

April
(30 days)

June
(30 days)

May
(31 days)

A whole year passes
between birthdays.
Joey's birthday is in January.
This year he will be 6.

Is his birthday in Spring, Summer, Autumn or Winter?

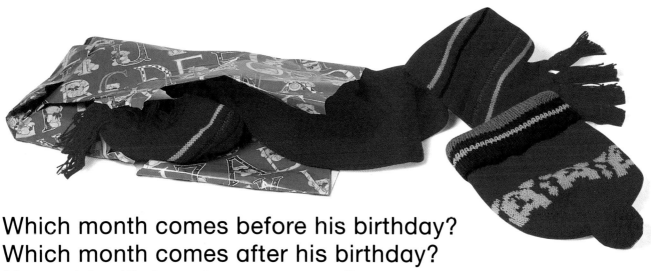

Which month comes before his birthday?
Which month comes after his birthday?
How old will Joey be next year?

Ask the same questions about your birthday.

A day to remember

On your birthday, make a form like this
and fill it in. Take a photo too.

My birthday is on October 12.
I am _____ years old.
I am _____ centimetres tall.
I weigh _____ kilograms.
My shoe size is _____.

Do the same next year and see
how much you have grown.

Clocks everywhere

Often we need to know how long it takes to do something or what time of day it is.
We measure time with clocks.

Look out for clocks and you will see them everywhere you go.

An alarm clock wakes you up in the morning.
What other helpful jobs do these clocks do?

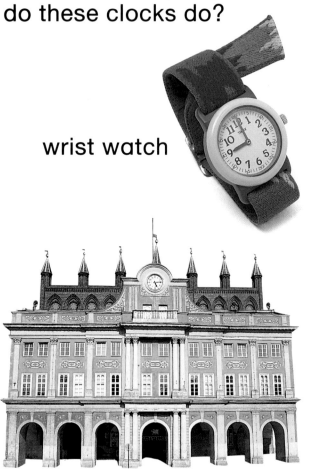

wrist watch

alarm clock

town hall clock

oven clock

children's clock

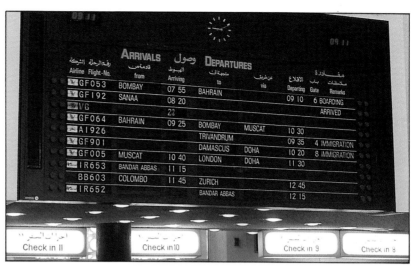

airport clock

ARRIVALS وصول				DEPARTURES مغادرة				
Airline Flight-No. رقم الرحلة الشركة	from قادمة من	Arriving الهبوط		to متجهة إلى	via عن طريق	Departing الإقلاع	Gate باب	Remarks ملاحظات
GF053	BOMBAY	07 55		BAHRAIN				
GF192	SANAA	08 20				09 10	6	BOARDING
I/G		2?						ARRIVED
GF064	BAHRAIN	09 25		BOMBAY	MUSCAT	10 30		
A1926				TRIVANDRUM		09 35	4	IMMIGRATION
GF901				DAMASCUS	DOHA	10 20	8	IMMIGRATION
GF005	MUSCAT	10 40		LONDON	DOHA	11 30		
IR653	BANDAR ABBAS	11 15						
BB603	COLOMBO	11 45		ZURICH		12 45		
IR652				BANDAR ABBAS		12 15		

Check in 11   Check in 10   Check in 9   Check in 8

station clock

Optimum Picture Control

clock on a video recorder

A clock measures time in hours, minutes and seconds.

Clock watching

You might be late for school if you didn't know the time.

How many other things in your day might you miss if you didn't know the time?

Seconds

A second is a very small amount of time.
It takes about 1 second to clap once or
to stamp your foot.

Here are some things to do that take about 1 second.
Try them and see.

1 bounce of
a ball

1 bang on a
drum

1 skip with
a rope

1 swallow of
water

What else can you do that
takes about 1 second?

These timers measure seconds ticking by.

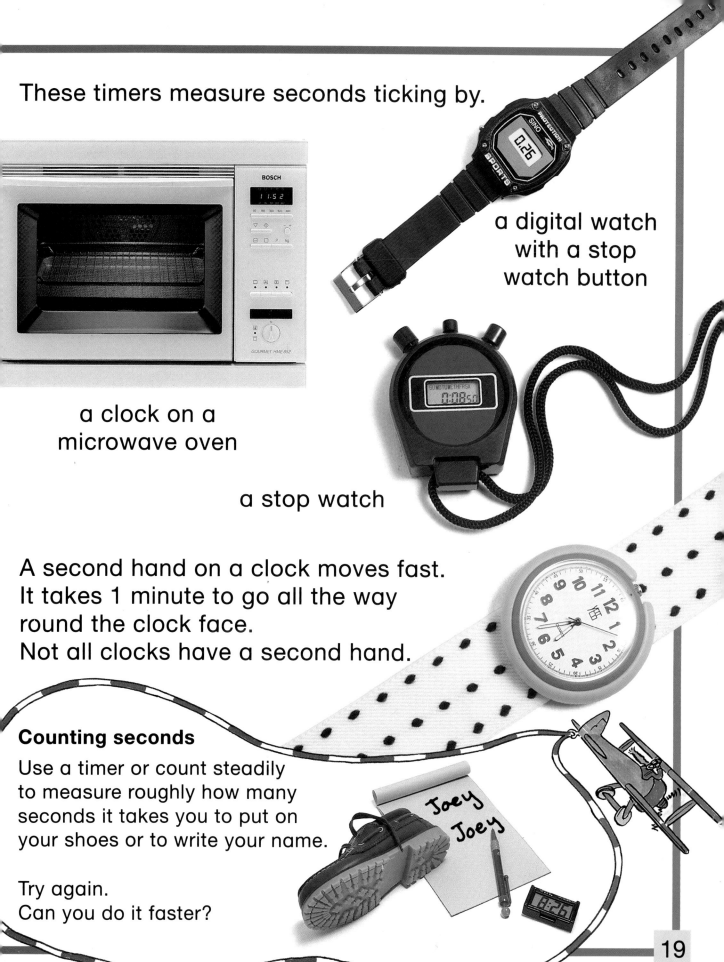

a digital watch
with a stop
watch button

a clock on a
microwave oven

a stop watch

A second hand on a clock moves fast.
It takes 1 minute to go all the way
round the clock face.
Not all clocks have a second hand.

Counting seconds

Use a timer or count steadily
to measure roughly how many
seconds it takes you to put on
your shoes or to write your name.

Try again.
Can you do it faster?

Minutes and hours

There are 60 seconds in 1 minute.

This is the minute hand on a clock. It goes too slowly to see it move.

It takes 1 minute to move this far round the clock.

These are the minutes on a digital clock.

You can see them change every time a minute passes.

It takes 1 minute to take your temperature.
It takes 10 minutes to hard boil an egg.

There are 60 minutes in 1 hour.
It takes the minute hand 1 hour
to move all the way round
the clock.

This is the hour hand
on a clock.

It moves even more slowly
than the minute hand.
It takes 1 hour to move from
one number to the next.

This number tells you
the hour on a digital clock.

It takes the small hand 12 hours
to go all the way round the clock.

There are 24 hours a day, so it
goes round twice each day.

The small hand points at the 12
at midnight and midday.

An hour is a long time.
Notice what you are doing during
the day as the hours pass.

Telling the time

The position of the hands on a clock face tells you the time.

When the minute hand is pointing to the 12, it is something o'clock.

The hour hand is pointing to the 4.

Both hands together tell you it is 4 o'clock.

The numbers on a digital clock tell you the time.

When the minute number shows 00, it is something o'clock.

The hour number is 4.

Both numbers together tell you it is 4 o'clock.

Try telling the time on these clocks.
Do any of them show the same time?

Clock hands always follow the numbers in order around the clock. We call the direction they move in clockwise.

We often divide hours up into halves and quarters.

The minute hand has moved quarter of the way round the clock face. The hour hand is just past the 4. We say the time is now quarter past 4.

The minute hand has moved half way round the clock. The hour hand is halfway between the 4 and the 5. We say it is half past 4.

The minute hand has moved three quarters of the way round the clock. It has a quarter still to go. The hour hand is nearly on the 5. We say it is quarter to 5.

Moving hands

What number does the minute hand point to

- when it is quarter past something?

- when it is half past something?

- when it is quarter to something?

Passing minutes

It is 4 o'clock.

One minute goes by.

The minute hand has moved 1 minute past 4 o'clock.

It takes the minute hand 5 minutes to move between each number on the clock face.

Put your finger on the blue 5.
Move it clockwise round the clock counting the minutes in 5s.

The time on this clock is 5 minutes past 4 o'clock. We say it is 5 past 4.

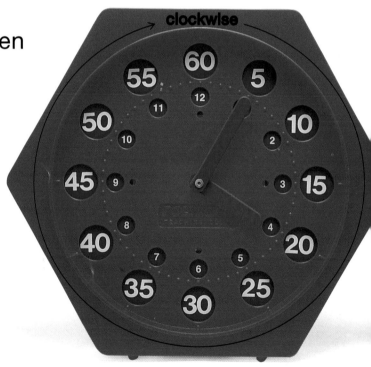

What is the time on this clock?
5 past 4. It is the same.
Were you right?

Tell the time as the minute hand moves around the clock face.

The digital clock is showing the same time.

four ten
(4:10)

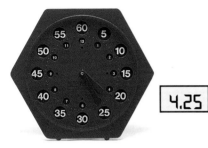

four twenty-five
(4:25)

four forty
(4:40)

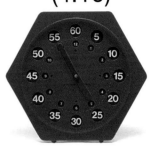

four fifty-five
(4:55)

Before clocks were invented, people used other things to measure time.

Hands and numbers

Point to the place the minute hand would be on a clock face when a digital clock shows these times:

4:15   4:30   4:45.

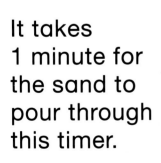

It takes 1 minute for the sand to pour through this timer.

It takes 1 hour for the shadow to move from one number to the next on this sundial.

How long does it take?

Joey started to make his sandwich at 3 o'clock.

He finished making it at 5 past 3.

The minute hand moved 5 minutes round the clock while he was making his sandwich.
He took 5 minutes.

How long did Joey take to do all these things?

Joey took
- 20 minutes to do his painting
- 30 minutes to build his castle
- 15 minutes to finish his jigsaw.

Were you right?

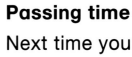

Passing time

Next time you clean your teeth, get dressed or eat your breakfast, look at the clock to see how long you take.

Find out how long you take to do some other things.

What is the time?

The time can be written as words or numbers.
Can you read the times written on this page?
Follow the string from each word to see if you are right.

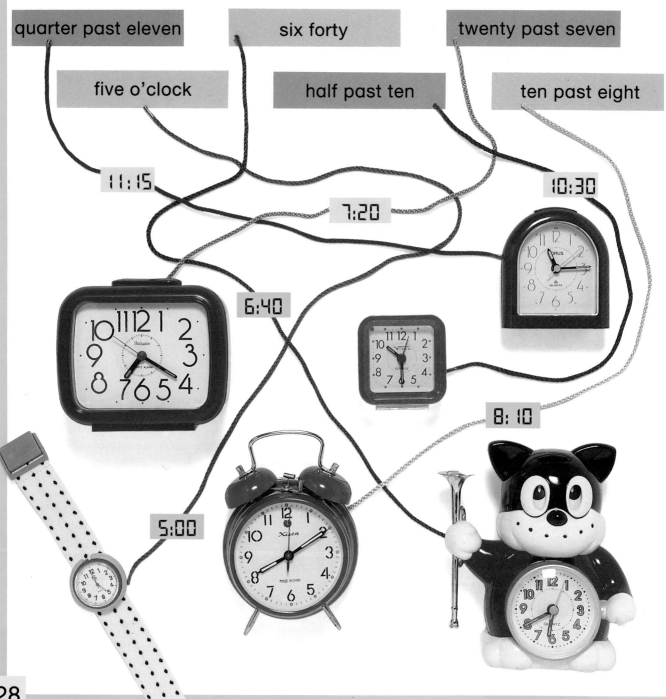

quarter past eleven

six forty

twenty past seven

five o'clock

half past ten

ten past eight

11:15

7:20

10:30

6:40

8:10

5:00

Make a clock

Use the clock face and hands on this page to make a clock. It will help you practise telling the time.

1 Trace the clock face and hands with the tracing paper. Do not trace the numbers.

2 Rub the traces down on to the card. Cut the face and hands out.

3 Go over the minute marks with the felt-tip pen so they are easy to read.

4 Now write on the numbers. Be careful to put them in the right place.

5 Fix the hands to the middle of the clock face with a paper fastener.

6 Move the hands and tell the time!

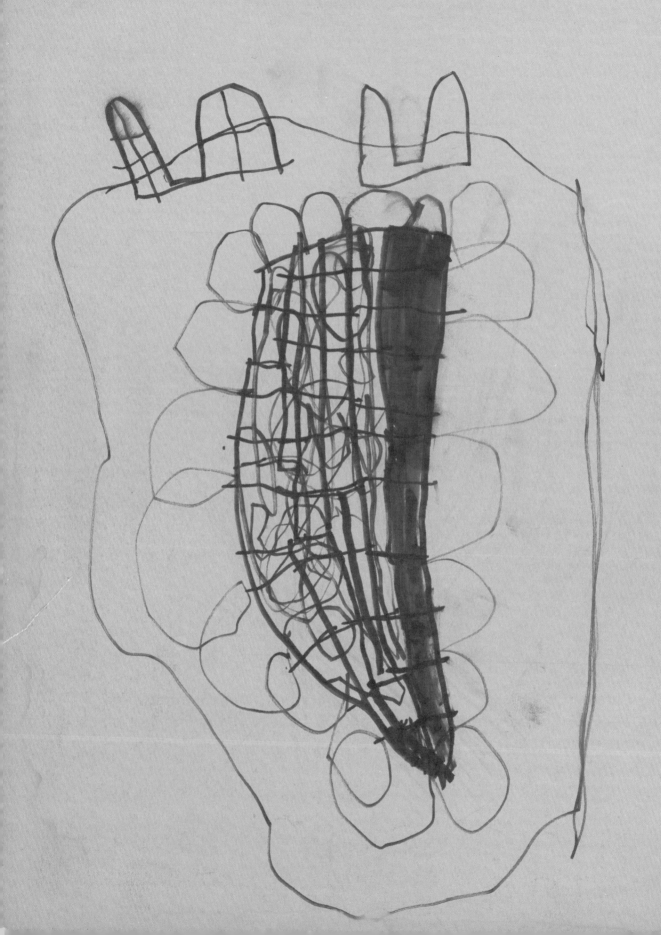